# CROWN YOUR KING

## MAKE THE BEST MOVE

# DR. BLANCHE PENN

# CONTENTS

# INTRODUCTION
## CROWN YOUR KINGS

I can remember when I would play spades with my siblings. I would eagerly anticipate the opportunity to obtain the ace of spades, as I was confident it would secure my victory. But what I did not think about was how I would play the game to win. In life, sometimes we play games and are not sure of the outcome of the game. However, the community leaders who have worked in our community understand how to play the game to succeed and support others who need their services. However, in life, we still need to reflect on the outcome, objectives, and goals to be successful. As I began to research more about the games we play and the people we meet every day, I thought these men in the community were not Kings, rulers of any state or county, lords, princes, overcomers, or chiefs of any state, heads of groups, no crowns but individuals that serve the community in our cities and towns. However, they were strong Black leaders who served people and individuals in the community. If our leaders were dukes, kings of states, governors, and commanders, would they still serve the community? And if these men were KINGS, would they still respect the community and serve in what roles? We can ask questions all day, but we will get the answer that we like to hear or know the answers that we would get for that question. As a writer, it was important for me to describe these gentlemen as I did with the Queens Forever book (Greatness Under the Rock). I initially believed that saying "Kings Forever" would be a simple task. However, as I delved into the subject matter, I quickly realized the complexity of the task. I found myself contemplating the numerous exceptional male leaders within our community in order to find the perfect title for this book. The male community leaders in our community play vital roles as grassroots organizers, not-for-profit organizations, and business owners. As I begin to reflect on my experiences and understand the roles of significant men, it becomes apparent that certain men and leaders often go unnoticed in literary works; I am reminded of men of the past, future, and present in our community. Reflecting on the challenges that so many men have faced, I decided it was time to honor these heroes in our community. These strong Black men are like cultural icons in the community.

Many nations have strong men in their communities, yet many of these individuals go unacknowledged as heroes. Even if we can't change what has happened or what will happen, we can wish the best for all men who have contributed to our world and community. In this book, I will mention a few people who have contributed to the modernization of many people's lives; however, you might not be familiar with them. Please take pleasure in learning more about these unsung heroes as I continue the journey of reflection on them.

# CHAPTER 1

# Men In Our City Are Moving

Changing times requires changing the perspectives of many individuals who live, work, and play in the community and do not know many of the unsung heroes in their community. My next statement was important to add to the timeline, as it sheds light on the unfortunate reality that numerous Black males are being denied equitable housing opportunities, thus hindering their ability to support their families. I was in a City Council meeting on Monday, 8/29/23, when I ran into a young man who was waiting to see if his nonprofit organization would get the funding for his project. Before I tell you about my encounter with this young man, let me tell you why I was down there. The city is always changing the rules; initially, one could speak for three minutes. However, now they have reduced it to a mere 2 minutes. To make matters worse, there were fifteen individuals scheduled to speak, and I found myself on the waiting list, second to last. Now, you know I was hot. But it was God stepping in to make sure I would speak on housing. To cut a long story short, about six or seven of the fifteen did not come to speak. My subject was housing, but every time I asked one of the city councils' members or the mayor about housing, they would tell me the AM I. Clearly, I was completely ready for them. The term 'area median income' (AMI) refers to the middle-income level for families within a particular geographic region. AMI is pivotal in formulating housing policies and assessing qualifications for different housing initiatives. Additionally, I stated that hearing 'AMI' once more would drive me up the wall. Here is my AMI.

- AM I – going to get fair housing?
- AM I – for the youth in our community?
- AM I – going to be able to have a place to live, work, and play?
- AM I – making money to pay for my house?
- AM I – You know the rent is too damn high?
- AM I – going to get those junk fees?
- AM I – going to be safe in my community?
- AM I – going to get a good landlord?
- AM I – going to have good healthcare?
- AM I – helping disabled people?
- AM I – helping our seniors have a place to stay?
- AM I – AM I – look. All we want is fair housing for all.

I have shared all this to introduce someone at the meeting who has dedicated himself to serving our community. His story is not mine to tell, as he will share it in his own words. I invite Greg Jackson to join me on this stage, a person I encountered during the events following the Keith Lamont Scott shooting in 2016. He has successfully secured a grant from the city.

# Greg Jackson

Greg Jackson, 2021 Charlottean of the Year and father of three girls, was a rapper and a sous chef when protests began following the Keith Lamont Scott shooting in 2016. Greg led a group to protest at the Charlotte-Mecklenburg Police Department headquarters. A crucial conversation that day changed his  trajectory. Shortly after, he started the nonprofit Heal Charlotte. Through Heal Charlotte, Greg has helped train officers to communicate with the community in volatile situations, created an after-school camp for at-risk youth in his northeast Charlotte neighborhood of Orchard Trace Condominiums, and deployed efforts that focused on revitalizing the area with a holistic approach to the family unit. Serving the community and being a bridge of communication between the community and its officials is what drives him. In his words, "If everybody did a little, no one would have to do a lot."

# Keith Grimes

Originally from Shelby, NC, and having lived in Charlotte for most of his life, Keith most recently worked as a casualty operations assistant/case manager for the North Carolina Army National Guard at Joint Forces Headquarters in Raleigh, NC. Keith served in the United States Army, the United States Coast Guard, and the North Carolina Army National Guard. Keith was deployed to Kuwait in 2019 and was further deployed to a combat zone in Saudi Arabia for six months before returning home to Charlotte in August 2020. Keith's combined military service allowed him to retire from the military in May 2023 after an impressive 20 years of service. Past employment for Keith includes eight years as a Recreation Center Assistant with Mecklenburg County Parks and Recreation, three years as a Human Services Specialist with Mecklenburg County Department of Social Services, and 13 years as a Senior Admissions Specialist with Central Piedmont Community College. Keith has a Bachelor of Arts degree in History and a Master of Arts degree in Military Studies from American Military University. He is married to Angela, and they have two adult children (Francis and Keith Jr.) and one child nearing adulthood (Keith III).

# Jervay "JKnowTruth" Vanderhors

The Award-Winning Promoter of the Year, JKnowTruth, has taken the East Coast by storm with his innovative, ground-breaking marketing, promoting, and event planning concepts. He is a creative, passionate, and diligent young man who has mastered every entity he engages in. Jervay ("JKnowTruth") Vanderhorst is a native of Charleston, SC, but grew up in Charlotte, NC.

JKnowTruth is an individual who believes in "taking your destiny into your own hands." He's a businessman, an entrepreneur, and the CEO of Success Driven Enterprises (SDE), which debuted in 2001. SDE is a promotions and marketing company based Charlotte, NC. Using creative marketing strategies and promoti JKnowTruth has helped launch careers for artists such as 50, Piles, Floetry, Akon, Young Jeezy, Eve, and several othe Recently, he was blessed with the opportunity to join Harvey Neighborhood Awards team in Las Vegas, NV He was also honored to work under the umbrell legendary Dick Clark Productions Super Bowl W annual NFL Honors. Other notable events wor Hip Hop Awards (Miami), Black Girls Rock Awards (Los Angeles), Nickelodeon's Kid's Angeles), NBA Allstar Weekend, Latin Latin Billboard Awards (Miami), ESP Honors (DC.) BET Awards (Los Ange (Atlanta), and BET Celebration of G

only a CEO and promoter but also an event coordinator/host. JKnowTruth is highly requested because he brings life to any event.

# Earl Owens

I am actively involved in the community. I have spent the past two years helping to educate the community on the dangers of COVID-19. I have worked at testing and vaccination sites, setting them up and organizing events with the communities. I am also on the board of the Mecklenburg Council of Elders. I work with 100 Black Men, Time Out Youth, Running Works, A Roof Above, 24/7 Dad, Youth Development Promises, Exodus House, Promise Resource Network, among others. My experience is as a certified peer specialist for Genesis Project 1. Case management through support systems advocacy. I'm tasked with linking clients to resources that can improve their quality of life. My experience extends to the Mental Health First Aid Certification, Mental Health Technician Certification, and Community Health Worker Center for Community Transitions / NC-FIT. I also connect people returning to the community with medical treatment; provide resources for medications, mental health treatment, and substance use treatment; help navigate employment and housing; and provide resources for community activities and programs that continue to introduce people back into the community.

## Education

- GED
- West Virginia Adult Education Center – Glenville, WV 2008

- Central Piedmont Community College – Charlotte, NC
- NC Peer Support Ongoing Training (PSS.NC.EDU)
- CPSS, CMHT, CHW, CLC, QP, FPS

## Skills

- Street smarts and extensive criminal/gang behavior assessment, mental wellness evaluation, and substance use detection (10+ years)
- Behavioral Health
- Developmental Disabilities Experience
- Case Management
- Behavioral Health
- Group Therapy
- Tattooing
- Behavioral Therapy
- Motivational Interviewing
- Crisis Intervention
- Microsoft Office
- Social work
- Management
- Customer service
- Supervising experience

# Mitch Patterson, also known as DJ Blessed

djblessed704@gmail.com (704) 904-2881

Mitch Patterson, also known as DJ Blessed, is the most popular DJ in Charlotte, North Carolina. With a military background, his loyalty and discipline are displayed greatly throughout the church and community! As an active member of the Gospel Industry Network, he is the gospel hip-hop advisor. He is also a member of The Heights Ministry in Charlotte, NC, and a valuable team  leader of the Pillow Talks w/Katris Wright on iheartradio LLC. He is paving the new way for gospel hip-hop music. DJ Blessed is a movement all by himself. He continues to be a man after God's own heart. He loves to worship and praise, and he has performed and ministered before large and small crowds during his career. Nominated for "Queen City's Award for two consecutive years as DJ of the Year, received the Charlotte "Community DJ of the Year 2021, and was the recipient of the "Black Father's Rocks" Activist of the Year award in 2021. Mitch Patterson (DJ Blessed) keeps his foundation strong by staying close to his loving wife, Rev. Patrina Patterson, three awesome adult children, seven grandchildren, and two great-grandchildren. DJ Blessed will inspire and encourage you through the diversity of styles of music that he mixes and releases. Mitch is a man of God who ministers through his work. Available for all types of events and will impress you on all professional levels.

# Kevin Hayes

## *Michael Jackson Impersonator*

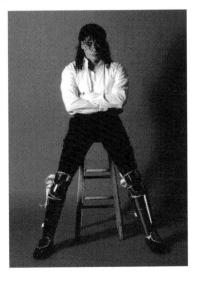

For 26 years, Kevin has been busy perfecting his craft and learning various dance styles like African, Jazz, Salsa and Tap. His own style of dance is influenced and inspired by Boogaloo Shrimp, Chris Brown, Channing Tatum, Sammy Davis, Jr., James Brown, Janet Jackson, Levelle Smith Jr, Michael Jackson, Pavan Thimmiah, Shabba Doo, and Usher. He has danced for the stars from the East Coast to the West Coast. He has opened up for Busta Brown Summer Festival, CIAA Half-Time Show (1998), Doug E. Fresh, Kid n'Play, Ki Ki Sheppard (Tribute to Roger Troutman), N-Tyce, Outkast and Wu-Tang Clan. He has auditioned for America's Got Talent (2014) and Showtime at the Apollo (2015), Beyonce World Tour (2006), 102 Jamz Crew and Mr. Bill Productions.

## Corporate Events
MICHAEL JACKSON IMPERSONATOR
Family Night
QUEEN CHARLOTTE FAIR, Concord, NC

Zeta Phi Beta Regional Leadership Convention
JOSEPH S. KOURY CONVENTION CENTER, Greensboro, NC

*Dr. Blanche Penn*

Michael Jackson Tribute Show
VENUE@1801, Charlotte, NC

Village of Clemmons Lip Sync Battle
SOUTHWEST ELEMENTARY SCHOOL, Clemmons, NC

NYE 2019 Celebration
VILLAGE INN EVENT CENTER, Clemmons, NC

Scarowinds Monster Block Party
CAROWINDS, Charlotte, NC & Fort Mill, SC

End of the Summer Block Party
A & K's CAFÉ, Greensboro, NC

Stop the Violence Rally
DESTINY TEMPLE, Winston-Salem, NC

UBAANA 13th Annual Convention Conference
EMBASSY SUITE, Charlotte, NC

Friendly People Who Cares
NOVANT HEALTH, Winston-Salem, NC

The Oaks at Forsyth
NOVANT HEALTH, Winston-Salem, NC

National Dental Health Association Convention
KINGSTON PLANTATION, Myrtle Beach, SC

Universoul Circus 25<sup>th</sup> Anniversary Tour
EASTLAND MALL, Charlotte, NC

Game Bus Party
Virginia Beach, Va

Halftime Is Gametime Battle of the Bands
ESPN, Fayetteville

Michael Jackson Tribute Band Artist Show
CAROWINDS, Charlotte, NC /Fort Mill, SC

Konnected Magazine Tenth Annual Queen City Awards
Ceremony
CHARLOTTE OASIS SHRINERS, Charlotte, NC

Johnson C. Smith 2017 Homecoming Parade
JOHNSON C. SMITH UNIVERSITY, Charlotte, NC

Heroescon 2017
CHARLOTTE CONVENTION CENTER, Charlotte, NC

EOC Pep Rally
COOK ELEMENTARY SCHOOL, Winston-Salem, NC

I-95 Annual Truck Jamboree
I-95 TRUCK STOP, Kenly, NC

FAMOUS Restoration Runway
RESTORATION PLACE COUNSELING, Greensboro, NC

North Carolina A&T 2016 Homecoming Parade
NORTH CAROLINA A&T UNIVERSITY, Greensboro, NC

105.3 FM Michael Jackson Birthday Tribute
RADIO ONE, Charlotte, NC

Triad Barbecue Festival
AKA ENTERTAINMENT MEDIA, LLC., Winston-Salem, NC

Jaycees Christmas Parade
WINSTON-SALEM JAYCEES HOLIDAY PARADE, Winston-Salem, NC

WSSU 2015 & 2016 Homecoming Parade
WINSTON-SALEM STATE UNIVERSITY, Winston-Salem, NC

King Kingston's Who's Bad Concert
KINGSKIDS PROJECT ORGANIZATION, Winston-Salem, NC

National Black Theatre Festival
NC BLACK REPERTORY COMPANY, Winston-Salem, NC

104.5 FM Summer Fest
WCCG, Fayetteville, NC

# Brandon C. "Chuck" Brown

Brandon C. "Chuck "Brown, better known as Mr. Xcitement, was born in Florence, SC, and moved to Charlotte, NC, at 5 years of age. He spent the majority of his early life in private and Christian-based schools. He also attended two junior colleges, Louisburg College and Clinton Jr. College, but decided to do something outside of following in his parents' footsteps, both of whom attended HBCUs.

Chuck went on to create a faith-based organization in 2015 called Single Saved and Serious. It was formed to be a safe haven for singles to network and discuss their lifestyle outside of established churches. He then became involved with local community issues such as police brutality and youth violence. Chuck began supporting families of murdered offspring as these issues increased within the black, inner-city communities of Charlotte. After a short absence, he returned to the Charlotte Mecklenburg Schools system as a custodian in 2019. He immediately recognized that custodians needed a voice, someone who wasn't afraid to speak out about the lack of training, low morale, and stagnant wages. Glaringly, the lack of pay increases had put many custodians in a vulnerable situation as the cost of living increased in Charlotte. Chuck became a strong advocate, successfully winning the fight to increase hourly wages from $13 to $15 per hour during the COVID-19 pandemic.

Brandon "Chuck" Brown remains very passionate about decreasing the division between organizations and communities in Charlotte as well as between departments in the CMS school system. He continues to push for Building Services to develop a career path within Custodial and Environmental Services for those interested in vocational employment instead of going to college. He also continues to stay close to the residents and causes of Charlotte by hosting community, health, and social events with local music and artistic talent under the banner of "Mr Xcitement and Friends." Chuck is married and has an extended family of five children. On weekends, he can be found hosting and supporting local artistic and social events throughout the Charlotte Metro area.

# Aker Amun El Bey

Aker Amun El Bey is a multifaceted individual passionate about knowledge and committed to positive change in education and community engagement. With a background in the construction trades, mentoring, and mediation, Aker has dedicated his life to education, spiritual growth, and uplifting his community. Known as a leader amongst his peers, his nonprofit  organization, Community Participation and Revitalization Inc., was featured on the cover of the American Painting Contractor Magazine and at the 2022 PDCA National Painters and Decorators Convention in Orlando, Florida. Aker is a true advocate for workforce development and upward mobility for at-risk youth and adults. His organization also supports local seniors by offering paint therapy and meditation sessions in partnership with Humana Co. He also supports other local and international community organizations, including the Mecklenburg Council of Elders, Locked Out Love, and Be You Be Great, to name a few. Aker believes in giving back to the community at all costs and the importance of understanding our true history as indigenous American people. When not immersed in his work, he enjoys traveling, studying history, listening to good music, eating great food, and crystal mining. Aker's unwavering determination and dedication make him a driving force in his field, inspiring others to follow his path toward a brighter future.

# Anthony Thompson

I was born on December 5, 1977, to Maggie and Delta, in the beautiful city of Charlotte. I have a younger brother and sister. I grew up with my grandparents because my mother had me at a young age and because of her unpreparedness for the responsibilities of parenthood. I  had the opportunity to meet many children and older individuals during my frequent relocations in the 1980s. However, this constant movement instilled in me the importance of never becoming too comfortable. I am the father of three children. I had a wonderful childhood, but I complicated it by buying into the peer pressure of street life at a young age. I got into a lot of trouble until I finally went to prison in 1996. This was my awakening to knowledge of self and Black consciousness. After this, I came home and had social anxiety issues due to my confinement for seven years at the age of 18. I was federally charged in 2003 for firearm possession, and I served federal time for that. I came home in 2009 (I served a total of 18 years of my 46 years on prison plantations). I got married to my now ex-wife, and we had two beautiful children together. I owned a barbershop, a t-shirt line, a remodeling company, vending machines, and a janitorial service. This was my first introduction to what entrepreneurship was all about. I later founded a nonprofit organization called I Am Great Minds Inc., in 2016 to address the challenges faced by the youth in my community and the communities of Charlotte overall. I wanted to be a solution to a long, systematic problem that our youth and community at large face. So, this was the basis and/or idea behind I Am Great Minds Inc. – to be a catalyst for change. I went on to earn a paralegal degree and now a consultant in business and personal credit, helping people with business development. I Am Great Minds Inc. provides resources surrounding PTSD (Poverty Traumatic Stress Syndrome Disorder), health and wellness, research and development, and financial literacy. Growing up, I was never taught what I Am Great Minds Inc. has to offer, which are the tools to break the generational curses first and foremost.

# Ismaail Qaiyim Esq.

Ismaail Qaiyim is the principal attorney at the Queen City Community Law Firm. His commitment to providing high quality legal services to Charlotte's underserved populations stems from his own experiences growing up in West Charlotte. His unique background as a community  organizer, policy researcher, and freelance writer adds depth and clarity to his work as a community-based attorney. Ismaail was the recipient of the (2019 -2020) Berkeley Law Foundation Fellowship which enabled him to build a partnership with the Latin American Coalition. His work with the Charlotte Housing Justice Coalition has informed him of the needs of those who are facing eviction and are housing insecure. Ismaail is committed to the realization of housing as a human right. As a Charlotte Westside native, Ismaail is proud to serve his home city in the courtroom and on the ground.

In summary, throughout history, numerous individuals have been impacted by the presence of Kings in their daily lives. As time progressed, more and more Kings have emerged as influential figures in the everyday lives of the people they serve. There is much to ponder when reflecting on the vast array of events that have unfolded within our community since the dawn of time. Men play a significant role in our community due to the existence of both males and females since the beginning of time. As we continue our discussion with more of our Kings, I want to emphasize the importance of the men in our lives. They hold significance for all of us. Once you delve into the extensive biographies of these individuals, it becomes evident why they hold such significance within the community. Their impact as influential leaders is undeniable, making it crucial for us to continuously offer our support. Getting to know these community leaders is crucial, as they are individuals who are actively involved in your community, both professionally and personally.

# CHAPTER 2

# The Importance Of Knowing These Men

I concur with numerous scholars on the need for Black males to receive equitable outcomes in funding, housing, and more. This analysis will contribute to a conceptual framework and highlight the difficulties Black males encounter in obtaining funding. Despite varied studies on community engagement, there is a significant gap in male participation. Understanding the male viewpoint on this lack of involvement is crucial. Researchers agree that male involvement takes various forms, such as engagement in their children's education. However, the question remains whether many males in our community are overlooked for grants or funding compared to other organizations. I posit that without a deeper understanding of male involvement from their perspective, they will continue to be marginalized. Yet, many are actively contributing to the support of our communities. Thus, comprehending their narrative firsthand is vital.

While working on my degree, I frequently encountered Epstein's framework, which outlines six types of parental involvement: parenting, school communication, volunteering, home learning, school decision-making, and community collaboration. This framework has greatly enriched my understanding. If I were to expand on Epstein's framework, I would include the daily contributions of fathers, men, and leaders who support our community selflessly, seeking fairness for all. I'd like to mention my new acquaintance, whose mother, Ms. Betty, provides him with unwavering support. Mr. Cedric Lamonte Dean is indeed a prominent figure of the day.

# Cedric Lamonte Dean

CEDRIC LAMONTE DEAN (born June 14, 1972) is a formerly incarcerated author, activist, educator, real estate investor, and Criminal Justice Prevention professional practicing in all 50 states. Cedric is licensed to provide public health and welfare services in all 100 counties of North Carolina. Cedric Dean Holdings Inc. provides programs aimed at addressing specific reentry needs such as transitional housing, supported employment, financial stability, business, and home ownership.

He has gained recognition for his works such as "How to Stop the Killing," "How to Save Our Children from Crime, Drugs, and Violence," and "How to Stop Your Children from Going to Prison." Dean is the founder of Safeguard Atone Validate Educate (SAVE), a national 501(3)c organization dedicated to preventing lawlessness and building character in misguided minds. He is also the founder of Save a Child Month, an annual (New Year) initiative to make young people job-ready instead of jail-ready. In 2022, he started CEDRIC DEAN HOMES, a project dedicated to providing emergency transitional housing for returning citizens.

## EARLY LIFE AND BACKGROUND

Cedric Dean was born in Charlotte, NC, to a single-parent Christian mother. At 13 years old, he was re-birthed into a new world of crime, drugs, guns, and violence. He had a short-lived stint as an armed robber and drug dealer. When he was sixteen, he was charged and convicted of robbery with a dangerous weapon. This led to a significant period of time spent behind bars, totaling five and a half years. Eleven months after his release in February 1994, Dean found himself facing a six-count federal indictment. The charges included conspiracy to distribute crack cocaine and possession of a firearm by a convicted felon. He was convicted of the charges on May 20, 1996, and sentenced to life plus five years.

## AUTHOR

Seven years into his second prison term, Dean was placed in a special housing unit, where he was confined in a cell for 23 hours a day. With a lot of free time on his hands, he read an urban street novel entitled "B-More-Careful" by Shannon Holmes, an author who once served time in prison. He enjoyed the book so much that, after finishing it, he started writing his own story: "For the Love of the Streets." This was Dean's first literary work and was published in 2008. "Mine is the tale of someone whose faith in God, willingness to change, strength, and infatuation to overcome barriers, impediments, and unusual odds can be a blueprint for anyone on the path of (premature) death and self-destruction," Dean wrote in "How to Save Our Children from Crime, Drugs, and Violence," a self-help book published in 2010. "Cedric Dean has himself crossed over the threshold of crime and violence to become the advocate for responsive change in our youth," said author Eugene Linwood, founder of Reaching Out Beyond Bars. "I have proudly watched him mentor, teach and apply tough love to redirect the pain, fear and uncertainness of young prisoners into courage, dedication and commitment. Cedric has done what many people have tried to do with our youth, but you must walk the walk and talk the talk." When Dean entered the literary arena in 2002, he had very little to look forward to, serving life without parole. He read books on writing and studied the styles of established writers. He first enrolled in an inmate-taught creative writing class. He completed that and eventually taught a writing course of his own. "I was also not supposed to become a teacher and transform gangsters into gentlemen inside of prisons," Dean wrote, "but I made a promise to the people who helped me along the way that I would help others who are living like I used to live. I didn't think it was possible for someone with a past like mine to be given the opportunity to teach anyone anything." Dean's teachings have helped hundreds of prisoners obtain their General Education Diploma, and thousands more have changed their lives for the better. "His ability to focus his energy in a positive way has set an excellent example for many of the younger inmates who look to him as a leader," Lance Cole, a Federal Bureau of Prisons Supervisor of Education, said about "Dean's infectious energy and enthusiasm."

## SOCIAL REFORMER IN PRISON

Around 2004, at the age of 32, Dean took a teaching job at the United States Penitentiary (USP) in Coleman, Florida. This assignment was pivotal: it introduced him to character education methods, psychoanalysis, activism (he served as the executive director of NAACP Prison Branch 5135) and taking direct action to bring about social change. The work and experience with the NAACP were, without question, very significant in the development of Cedric's own ideas and direction, and all from a low-profile teaching appointment. Cedric's early specialization was prisoner analysis, in which his interest and research expanded following his transfer to USP Atwater (in California) in 2005, where he also engaged in activist work and taught GED and, later, life skills. His early work focused primarily on testing and extending Gandhi's theory in relation to the effect of truth and love as supreme values of human psychology, with a strong emphasis on how society affects childhood maturation. This research entailed detailed social activism and awakened him to the doctrine of non-violence and love, notably conducted in early 2006 with grieving gang members of the CRIPS, whose infamous co-founder, Stanley "Tookie" Williams, had been executed. These experiences especially helped Cedric realize that Gandhi's ideas lacked vital urban criminal dimensions and provided a key for his 'biopsychoactive' perspective. Cedric subsequently moved to four other United States penitentiaries, continuing his focus on prisoner welfare and eventually expanding his concentration to child welfare. He also created Save a Child Month in 2012 to address juvenile delinquency and treat trauma and mental illness. When the Sandy Hook Elementary School shooting devastated America, Cedric provided some key solutions to the surge in gun violence in his book, "How to Stop the Killing," which he released on the one-year anniversary (December 14, 2013). Despite being awarded a lesser security transfer, Cedric continued his research and writing, leading the largest prisoner-led movement in America - Safeguard Atone Validate Educate.

## COMMUNITY ACTIVIST

In 2009, Dean founded Safeguard Atone Validate Educate with the objective of helping all young people with academic, behavioral, and financial problems graduate from high school and become more employable. One year later, in 2010, he received the Federal Bureau of Prisons' highest award: the Call-to-Service

Award. He became the first United States Penitentiary Lee inmate to receive such an honor. He was known throughout the prison as "A Leader's Leader." In late 2010, Dean reached a wider audience by recording the first in a series of motivational speech presentations for the international media. "Here is a young man who is doing stuff out of prison that we are not even doing in our communities," said Janice Peak-Graham, radio host of 'Our Common Ground.' "We need 10 'Cedrics' in the community on the outside." He conducted online motivational counseling sessions not only for at-risk youth but also for the parents and teachers of at-risk youth. "This urgent call to action for each of us and for our country is to work with one another and government officials in our communities to find ways to make our communities safer and to foster positive relationships with our children," Dean said in his "I have a Plan" speech. "My plan will SAVE - safeguard, atone, validate, and educate our children. With this plan, we will be able to teach our children how to live side-by-side and deal with their differences without malice or violence. With this plan, we will take major steps to substitute the pipeline to prison for a pipeline that will bring prosperity to many of our children." In 2017, Cedric was released after serving 22 years and 11 months. Since his release, he has given motivational speeches in 39 of the 50 states, including his appearances at the 2019 State of the Union Address and the 2021 Oscar Awards.

## BOOKS

Dean details his life and the relationships that have helped reshape it in his 20 published books. Much more than an average incarcerated author, Dean's life-saving books, which are divided into a series of written exercises in workbooks, focus on areas of peer pressure - such as bullying, anger management, and misguided thinking - as well as on areas of self-worth, such as self-confidence, courage, and character. "I applaud you, even while serving time in prison, for stepping up and taking responsibility for helping find a solution," Kevin Jennings, former assistant deputy secretary of education, wrote to Dean in 2010. In 2011, Dean collaborated with the Federal Bureau of Prisons and launched a replica of his SAVE program called RISE (Rehabilitate, Integrate, Stimulate, and Educate). "The hearts, souls, and minds of each of you can rise," Dean wrote in a message to the misguided. "Power is in your ability to use your mind. The more you think, the more powerful you become."

SELF-HELP BOOKS

How to Stop Your Children from Going to Prison (2008)

Leaders Breed Leaders (2009)

How to Save Our Children from Crime, Drugs, and Violence (2010)

Born Leaders (2011)

How to Stop the Killing (2013)

My Mother, My Best Friend (2018)

NEW LIFE CURRICULUM WORKBOOKS

Controlling Your Thoughts (2011)

Overcoming Peer Pressure (2011)

Anger Management (2011)

Solving Social Problems - Bullying (2011)

New Hope (2011)

ADULT WORKBOOKS

How to Stop Your Children from Going to Prison (2011)

Leaders Breed Leaders (2011)

SAVE's Effective Communication Curriculum (2014)

FICTION For the Love of the Streets (2008)

Pimping in the Name of the Lord (2008)

Operation Con-Freedom (2008)

## 5-LEVEL PARADIGM OF PEACE

1. Goodwill - kindness, compassion, sympathy

2. Genuineness - honesty, acceptance, contrition, consideration

3. God-fearing - faithful, trustworthy, devoted, honorable, virtuous

4. Gracefully - balanced, dignified, self-respecting, diplomatic, prudent

5. Gradually - step-by-step, bit-by-bit, forward-looking, ducks in a row. "We must practice each principle simultaneously, emphasizing the third, which deals with the most significant for the procurement of peace," Dean said about the 5-level Paradigm of Peace. He gave these examples in use: "You can't achieve peace when you have goodwill (level 1, but you're not God-fearing (level 3), which represents the CENTER of the five principles. You can be honest (level 2), but you must also be prudent (level 4) in your pursuit of peace."

# Gemini Boyd

Gemini Boyd was born and raised in Charlotte, NC, and was released from federal prison in 2016 after serving 20 years. While incarcerated, he noticed the prisoners coming in were getting younger and younger. He also started to reminisce about his own experience and wondered if he  would have had someone in his life to guide him down the right path and if he would be in his current situation. Gemini made up his mind that once he was released from prison, he would do everything in his power to make a difference in the lives of members of his community.

Since his release, Gemini has focused on amplifying the issues of the marginalized community and collaborating with others to have a greater impact on bringing about change. He is currently a consultant to the Public Defender's Office and a member of Leadership Charlotte Class 44. Gemini's accomplishments include a Youth Town Hall Forum that created a platform for high school students to share their experience with school violence and Charlotte Day 2019, a community event focused on unity and how it can decrease violence in our city. He understands that it is not just about a second chance but a better chance, and he has committed his life to a better chance for all.

# Kenny Robinson

Kenny Robinson is the founder and executive director of Freedom Fighting Missionaries (FFM), a nonprofit organization dedicated to assisting formerly incarcerated and justice-involved individuals and their families. After serving 10 years in federal prison and being released to Charlotte, NC, Kenny  experienced firsthand the challenges faced by those reentering society. Despite struggling to find employment and basic resources, Kenny persevered and secured a job at Goodwill, earning a meager wage of $7.25 per hour. Through hard work and determination, Kenny rose through the ranks and became a top salesman at a local Mazda car dealership. He was eventually promoted to finance manager and then sales manager. He used his position to provide opportunities for others with similar backgrounds. Kenny became renowned in the community for offering second chances to those in need. In December 2019, Kenny retired from the car dealership and founded FFM. Together with a small team of dedicated volunteers, he created a reentry program that leverages their lived experiences. FFM focuses on four key areas of basic need resources: identification, healthcare, employment, and affordable housing. The organization has experienced remarkable growth, now employing a staff of eight and raising millions of dollars.

Their efforts have assisted thousands of individuals, making FFM the first reentry organization to receive Section 8 housing vouchers. Kenny Robinson's journey is truly inspiring and serves as a testament to the power of perseverance and support in overcoming the challenges of reentry. By seeking support from organizations that assist individuals with criminal records, Kenny was able to access resources and guidance that helped him navigate the complexities of reintegration. Attending job training programs not only equipped Kenny with new skills but also demonstrated his commitment to personal growth and development. By actively engaging in community activities, Kenny was able to rebuild his network and establish connections that played a crucial role in his successful reintegration. Kenny's story is a reminder that with determination, resilience, and the support of others, individuals with criminal records can overcome the barriers they face upon reentering society. His journey serves as an inspiration to others, showing that it is possible to rebuild one's life and create a brighter future, no matter the obstacles that may arise. Kenny, a proud father of seven children and grandfather of nine grandchildren, continues to be a community advocate for the justice-involved, homeless, and disabled. He actively serves on the Mecklenburg County Continuum of Care and chairs the Mecklenburg County Equity and Inclusion Committee. Kenny's unwavering commitment to equal rights drives his work and vision for expanding FFM's reentry model nationwide.

# Tommy L. Nichols

A multi-talented creative media and technology professional. Tommy Nichols is the CEO of Power Up USA, a technology, training, and events company that's closing the digital divide in underserved communities. He is the founder of the Charlotte Black Film Festival, the Queen City Arts Festival, and IOCTV, a 24-hour streaming network created to support African American content creators, which  was selected as the best streaming/virtual platform in Charlotte by Queen City Nerve. In addition, Tommy created the now 1400-member Carolina Black Film & Technology Collective, a monthly meetup that trains and equips African Americans in film and technology.

In 2020 and 2021, he was hired by the National Endowment for the Arts to review and recommend $4 million in grants to media arts organizations across the USA. In 2018, the mayor of Charlotte appointed him to the Charlotte Mecklenburg Public Access Corporation (TV 21)

board of directors, and he was board chair for the last three years of his two 3-year term that ended in June 2023. The Charlotte Black Film Festival has been a film screening partner of Sony, Lions Gate, Marvel, and Fox studios. Under his Tommy Filmworks brand, he was the media director for the winning campaigns of Charlotte City Councilwoman Dimpa Amera, Mecklenburg County Sheriff Gary

McFadden, and Mecklenburg County Judge C. Renee Little. He was the director of photography for Mattie, Johnny, and Smooth White Stone. Recently, he was given the opportunity to showcase his writing and directing skills as he was hired by the National Park Service to produce the history of African Americans in the Great Smoky Mountain.

With over thirty years of experience in Film and IT, Nichols was part of a $10 million computer and network integration project for Dayton Public Schools as well as the project manager of a $1.2 million dollar technology upgrade for the Department of Defense. Through his 501c3 organization, Power Up USA, Nichols has helped close the digital divide by providing technology and digital media training to over 3,200 youth, adults, and seniors. In 2024, anticipate the release of his book "Coding Black" and the launch of the Center for Digital Churches, a platform that helps the church use digital technology to empower the community they serve. He is also set to launch a job-matching website, reelnclusion.com, that promotes hiring minorities in the film and TV industry. In addition, he is the recipient of the Business Journal's 40 under 40, the YMCA Black Achievers Award, the Lifesaver Award from Kennedy Charter School, the 2019 Charlotte Black History Maker from WCCB TV, and was nominated for the Mayor's Educator Mentor of the Year Award.

In addition to his many awards, Nichols has been featured on ABC, NBC, FOX, CBS, the Charlotte Observer, the Charlotte Post, the National Publication Digital Journal, the cover of Pride Magazine Charlotte, and was recently selected by QC Metro as The Great 28: Black Charlotteans who are shaping our city. His experience and reputation in technology, film, and business have made him a sought-after consultant, speaker, and workshop presenter. He is a man of faith who is not ashamed of the Gospel of Jesus Christ; this is why he is passionate about loving people and closing the equity gap in all aspects of life.

# Robert Dawkins

Robert Dawkins is the Political Director for Action NC and the founder and state organizer for SAFE Coalition NC, which is a project of Action NC. This organization comprises over 15 community-based advocacy groups working to end discriminatory profiling and promote civil liberty protections for all North Carolina residents.

Before starting SAFE Coalition NC, Robert worked for 7 years with Democracy North Carolina as the Western NC Field Organizer, where his work centered on organizing communities of color on the issues of voter rights, voter access, and ending voter disenfranchisement. Robert was the head organizer for the Charlotte chapter of ACORN for 3 years. He worked in low- to moderate-income neighborhoods, building neighborhood capacity, neighborhood power, and leadership development.

Robert has a BA in Political Science from the University of South Carolina and a Graduate Certificate in Nonprofit Management from the University of North Carolina Charlotte.

# Michael T. Sanders

Michael T. Sanders hails from Pineville, NC. He currently teaches middle and high school instrumental music, choral music, and AP Music Theory at John Taylor Williams Secondary Montessori in Charlotte, NC. This is his sixth year at Williams  Montessori and his nineteenth year in public school music education. Mr. Michael T. Sanders earned a Bachelor of Music Education from UNCG, where he studied Music Education and the French Horn. He previously taught band at Lexington Middle School (NC), Durham School of the Arts in Durham, NC, Northwest School of the Arts, and Winterfield Elementary School in Charlotte, NC. Additionally, since 2011, he has been a teaching artist for the Charlotte Symphony Orchestra's Project Harmony, a collaboration between the Charlotte Symphony Orchestra and Arts+, formerly Community School of the Arts, targeting grades 2-5 instrumental music instruction. Now in its fifth summer, he is also the co-founder of the Greater Charlotte Summer Arts Camp, a camp geared for students ages 6-12 in visual and performing instruction. He is also a nineteen-year counselor and camp band conductor at the UNCG Summer Music Camp and a member of NCBA, NCMEA, NAfME, and Phi Mu Alpha Sinfonia. Sanders is currently a co-chair of the Charlotte-Mecklenburg Schools Middle School Honors Band, a representative of the East Learning Community on the Charlotte-Mecklenburg Schools Superintendent's Teacher Advisory Council, the Charlotte-Mecklenburg Schools AP Music Theory Lead Teacher, and a community advisory board member for Charlotte's own classical music radio station, WDAV. Sanders has also served as a guest clinician for several honor bands around North Carolina and coaches student musicians at local middle and high schools as well as the Charlotte Symphony Youth Orchestras. In his free time, he enjoys playing video games, repairing broken electronics, and hanging out with his family and friends.

# Chablis Dandridge

Chablis Dandridge is a Certified Peer Support Specialist with a special designation in the Forensic Peer Support curriculum. Chablis is a consultant on public safety issues with a focus on diversion, prevention, intervention, and restorative practices in the community of justice involved citizens. He is also a real estate professional specializing in working with the Greater Charlotte Metro Areas most underserved and vulnerable populations. Neighbors who are criminal justice involved, repeatedly unhoused, and those who face barriers to permanent housing because of mental health concerns is his focus and specialty. He is a thought leader in program planning, development, and implementation. He has worked in executive positions at numerous nonprofit organizations leading initiatives such as family skills building training to strengthen households and communities. He also speaks on human rights, social justice issues, and diversity, equity, and inclusion in the workplace. Chablis is the author of, "A Letter to My Sons, Leaving A Legacy of Love", which chronicles his journey of learning to embrace every moment to be the best, to be the catalyst for change, and to live life today as if it were your last.

In conclusion, as one King imparted to me, comprehending our viewpoints is crucial. While investigating various methods to foster partnerships and enhance male engagement, it was essential to connect with as many individuals as possible. Ultimately, the men in the community will take the lead in defining their roles in the games and deciding which move to make first.

# CHAPTER 3

# Which Move To Make First The Most Important Piece In The Game

I remember a time when I attempted to master the art of chess, but alas, my skills in the game were lacking. However, my son possessed a natural talent for it, so I continued to indulge in the game of checkers, where my abilities shone brightly. Mastering the art of moving the pieces is crucial to navigating the intricate world of our chosen craft. It's like solving a complex puzzle or engaging in a strategic game of chess where understanding the rules is key to achieving victory. I mention all of this to help you understand the piece we must move to thrive in this community. Now, it is time to play the game with the right piece to win. The attributes that support the male perspective are strong leadership skills, knowledge, patience, excellent work ethics, good listening ability, and outstanding communication skills. The characteristics of each of these males, coupled with their experiences and knowledge, will be helpful. Therefore, you will learn so much about them in their own words. Besides, when males build a healthy relationship, it is a win-win situation for everyone.

Understanding puzzles and chess can be a source of mental stimulation, inspiration, wisdom, humor, and a unique perspective on life. There have been moments when I've viewed life as a movie in which I play a role. However, it feels like the pieces are sometimes not aligned properly, resembling a game of chess or checkers or a puzzle missing a piece. Imagine viewing life as a puzzle, where each piece plays a crucial role in our journey. By strategically placing the right pieces together, could we ultimately triumph in this grand game? As we all know, every puzzle has its own unique challenge when a piece is missing. I remember when people were testing my knowledge of problem-solving a few issues. I began to think about a puzzle because when you play the game, the goal and intent are to solve the puzzles with all the pieces; if you do not have all the pieces, it might be difficult to finish the project. Despite everything, it was crucial for me to locate the final puzzle piece. Often, we fail to look down to see if it might be on the floor; we give up on solving the puzzle, but I persisted. It was beneath my foot, and with that, the puzzle was complete. I constantly remind my children to never stop until the task is finished. Now, without further ado, I would like to introduce you to more Kings in our community. Let's begin with Kareem, an extraordinary writer with a story you simply must hear. As one of the highlighted Kings of the hour, he possesses a unique way of sharing his insights. Kareem is set to broaden your perspectives, touch your soul, and captivate your heart with fresh revelations about life.

# KAREEM'Z BLOCK for CHRIST Community Development Mission!

Kareem'z Block For Christ Community Development Mission is focused on fostering spiritual enlightenment within our communities in the spirit of Jesus Christ. This community strives to address various needs, such as feeding the hungry, promoting economic empowerment, and fostering character development. Teaching and consulting sessions were conducted by members  of the community. For more information, please contact Soldier Kareem at 704-975-4185.

- Feeding The Hungry
- Educating The Community
- Mentoring The Youth


Soldier Kareem was known as the youngest member of the allegedly notorious West Charlotte Posse of Charlotte, NC. After being given "45 years" for his criminal endeavors, Kareem decided that the time had come to turn his life around for the better. Influenced by the spiritual teachings of Jesus and the autobiography of Malcolm X, Kareem went from being a thug to being a thinker. After serving 27 years, Kareem was released back into the community, where he now mentors' youth and dedicates his time and energy toward positive programs. Today, Kareem is an award-winning author from the Queen City of Charlotte. His books include his testimony, "Loved By The LORD, Hated By Satan!"; "Toya's Drama, Teenage Lust"; and "Your Daughter May Be A Thug!"

# Timmy Drayton

Timmy Drayton, affectionately known as Tim and Mr. Man, is celebrated for his unique fashion sense, the ensembles he sports, his expertise in modeling, and the ambiance he creates on the runway. His enthralling stare directed at the female spectators is legendary; reportedly, it has an almost melting effect on them. His signature slow turns on the catwalk is a spectacle in itself, reminiscent of a scene playing out in the deliberate tempo of slow-motion cinema. The narrative continues with the establishment of Mr. Man Fashion Company, founded by him on August 16, 1992. Currently, the company has fifteen models and goes beyond just fashion, it is committed to providing a range of community services. His professional goal is to use his skills and knowledge to mentor youth, teenagers, and seniors, proving that success in a modeling career is possible for those who pursue it. Timmy Drayton's original vision for Mr. Man Fashion Company was to offer guidance to those eager to learn about modeling. His experience includes serving as a lead model and fashion advisor at Paradise Fashion Company. He has also supported organizations like the Charlotte Post Scholarship Fund Inc., Kupperhelmer Men's Clothing Store, United House of Prayer for All People Church in Charlotte, Irby's Salon, and Myers Tabernacle A.M.E. Zion Church. A West Mecklenburg High School alumnus, he advanced his education at John Casablanca School with the goal of pursuing a career in fashion and modeling, earning accolades for perfect attendance, community service, and model of the year. Despite a busy schedule, Timmy Drayton also dedicates time to hobbies and activities such as swimming, reading, dancing, watching movies, and attending social events. Here are a few events that were so popular in the Queen City:

- Boulevard Homes: Coordinated youth fashion show classes for their community days.

- Greenville Center: Coordinated fashion classes and the crowing pageant of Mrs. Greenville.

- Youth Teen Group (off Beattie's Ford Road): Taught fashion classes for their First Year Anniversary Awards Banquet.

- Wilmore Community Parade.

- Bethlehem Center: Adopted a family for Christmas.

- Sugar Creek Center: Coordinated fashion classes.

- Thomas Jeffries Center: Coordinated fashion show and television program hosted by Helen Strong for African American People Magazine

- Pleasant Grove Baptist Church,

- Double Oak Community

- Davidson (YMCA), McCrorey Branch (YMCA)

Timmy Drayton has been a steadfast presence in the community, dedicating more than two decades to nurturing youth basketball teams and playing a significant role in the triumphs of award-winning squads at the local recreation centers.

# Joshua Bridges

Joshua Bridges has a mixed heritage, with American and Jamaican roots. Born and raised in Charlotte, NC, Joshua Bridges finished in the top ten of his class at West Charlotte and graduated from the University of North Carolina at Chapel Hill Kenan-Flagler Business School. He then joined the University of North Carolina at Chapel Hill football team and earned a full  scholarship. 2010 Academic All-American. He has been working in the nonprofit field since 2012. His first nonprofit work was in the Greensboro area, working with "The Benevolence Farm," a halfway house for women ex-cons to rehabilitate. He started the USK (University Soup Kitchen) on the campus of UNC Chapel Hill in 2013 and continued working in the professional and nonprofit worlds over the next decade. He has worked at big companies like Time Warner Cable, Red Ventures (where he became a master sales agent and managed hundreds of agents), Wells Fargo (Retirement specialist), Chime Solutions, and Spectrum, to name a few, while maintaining and expanding the University Soup Kitchen across this great state of North Carolina. Joshua Bridges has led voter registration drives, marches, and protests, and he fearlessly sat in the middle of uptown during the Keith Lamont Scott protest as they were tear gassed. He has fought against corporations and city officials, like Dilehay Courts, on behalf of gentrified and displaced communities in Charlotte. He has also walked on foot in almost every ghetto/impoverished area of this city and hand-delivered resources to people in need! In 2022, he became a licensed real estate agent and has continued to work in that field while serving the community. The University Soup Kitchen now serves over 1400 meals per month, as well as thousands of pounds of clothes, groceries, hygiene products, and more. They are a feet-on-the-ground grassroots group that delivers directly to the most underserved areas of the city. They have also served, fed, and clothed thousands of students and children in the Charlotte area and have provided jobs, rides, mental health resources, and more to many across this county. They now have six different campus chapters of student volunteers and leaders across North Carolina, including UNC Chapel Hill, UNCC, JCSU, CPCC, JWU, and Davidson.

# Ramon Augustus Hunsucker Sr

Ramon Augustus Hunsucker Sr. was born in Charlotte, NC, to Norris and Norma Hunsucker on January 24, 1976. I am the middle child of three children. I have two children, Makayla, who is 25, and Ramon Jr., who is 2. A son is also on the way. I am married to Petronila Hunsucker, my high school sweetheart, not knowing we would reconnect after 30 years. She brings with her my bonus kids and grandkids, so we have a great  blended family. I participated in a range of sports during my time in high school, including AAU basketball. This experience eventually led me to pursue basketball at Corning Community College in New York. Upon returning home, I decided to establish my own business called ASD. (Athletic Skills Development), which helps athletes develop skills or enhance what they already have in basketball. I am passionate about working with children and developing their skills in various sports. I love what I do. I attend Fire & Ice Ministries under the leadership of Pastor Darrius and Apostle Dana Williams. My motto is, "I live by God first, family second, and then me." I aspire to share my narrative with young boys, guiding them towards triumph in the face of challenges, peer pressure, and the complexities of life. I firmly believe that by prioritizing faith, one can always emerge victorious.

# Keith Sturghill

Keith Sturghill, a coach, author, and mentor based in Charlotte, North Carolina, dedicates his time to guiding K-12 students at multiple schools and recreation centers. With fifteen years of service at Mecklenburg Park and Recreation, he has been deeply involved in the community, organizing  teen summits, laser tag events, and a myriad of other youth activities.

# Rafael A. Penn

Rafael has always been fiercely independent, constantly on the move, and has a presence that's hard to ignore. Following in the footsteps of two siblings, he graced the stage in STAR with multiple performances. A talented gifted writer reminiscent of Petronila, Rafael has penned at least two songs for the production. His hobbies include  avid gaming and a knack for creating plays and videos. His work, "Ruffle Winners," gained particular attention. Known as SuperStarRalph on YouTube, he also served as a page in the General Assembly in Raleigh, North Carolina. Additionally, he played a significant role in a prominent legal case:

In the lawsuit involving Rafael Penn, Clifton Jones, and Donna Jenkins Dawson, they acted as plaintiff-intervenors against the Charlotte–Mecklenburg Board of Education, which was presented to the Supreme Court of North Carolina. The court found certain changes made by the General Assembly to the prekindergarten program unconstitutional. Specifically, two amendments were under scrutiny:

Subsection 10.7(f) was accused of restricting the percentage of "at-risk" children in the prekindergarten program.

Subsection 10.7(h) implemented a co-payment requirement for certain participants in the program.

# Charles Steveson

Charles has a passion for wrestling and community service. He has triumphed in numerous wrestling competitions and provides support for his mother and family. A man of few words, Charles, when he chooses to speak, shares generously about himself and his community.

# Felix Penn Maldonado

Felix A. Penn Maldonado has a way of motivating people with his smooth speech and captivating eyes that could make anyone swoon. In the STAR play, much like his sister, Felix shone brightly, delivering several song performances to rapturous applause and cheers from the audience, particularly the women, who were charmed when he tossed a flower during his performance. Additionally, Felix has collaborated with me to conduct

various workshops across multiple schools. Featured in the Winner PLUS Inc. brochure, he consistently strives to project a composed image. He is employed at the YMCA in Gastonia, North Carolina, where he is quite popular among the ladies and radiates a unique charm. He shares stories of visiting each supervisor's office, engaging them in conversation, all while maintaining a warm smile. When spending a considerable amount of time in one office, he courteously indicates that it's time to move on with his duties. So, ladies, when you see Felix, don't hesitate to greet him.

In conclusion, recognizing the importance of these remarkable men who become integral to anyone's life in a community is essential. Having explored and understood the aspects of male engagement in the community, it is vital to consider the main elements that foster effective organization and cooperation, which are necessary to bolster the Kings' associations within the community. The time has come to acquaint ourselves with more Kings in our community; search no more Kings have arrived.

# CHAPTER 4

# More Kings Have Arrived

I know you must be surprised that we have so many men working in the community. It is essential to learn from these individuals from a male perspective and examine their responses on how they would encourage more males to have businesses and nonprofit organizations and how to develop partnerships in the community. The males will provide an open dialogue for participants to honestly share their experiences and opinions to induce a change in their relationship with the city and county and to partner with other organizations. I can remember being on a board dedicated to supporting our community. We were actively involved in developing a new Meck PlayBook. However, it became evident that future updates and input from the community, nonprofit organizations, and grassroots organizations were necessary. But many of the Kings of organizations input was not a part of the development of that book. In the Meck Playbook (2021), the keywords that focus on partnerships are external partnerships, external organizations, formalized partnerships, increased accessibility, local communities, creative thinking, and quality programming. However, the MPB (2021) states, "establishing partnerships with existing private, public, and nonprofit organizations is the most cost-effective way to expand programs" (p. 156). Partnerships can come in many shapes, forms, and sizes. Therefore, collaborating and partnering with other organizations will prove to be cost-effective for the organization and MCPR.

According to the MPB (2021), "partnerships can be one-sided, as organizations look to use county-owned property for singular and particular uses. This can be precarious if the use is not open to the larger community and limited to a particular school, sport, or activity" (p. 154). Park and Recreation has room for improvement in terms of collaborating and establishing stronger relationships with grassroots organizations and nonprofits. According to MPB (p. 154), "enhance partnership protocols to ensure all parties are operating from a clear understanding of delivery requirements" (p. 154). The MPB also stated, "Mecklenburg Park and Recreation is eager to engage in partnerships with diversified groups and build community" (p. 155). Nevertheless, if the statement is true that MCPR engages in partnerships with diversified groups, it would be cost-effective and bring more organizations to the table as partners. I disseminate this information due to the necessity for enhanced backing from our county governments for grassroots entities and individuals from underserved communities. Numerous such organizations are upheld and operated by Black males. Adopting a more inclusive strategy, we forge a path toward a more promising future for our city, where the betterment of all lives and the collective prosperity of the community are realized.

After discussing the city at length, it's time to focus on its influential figures. The investments made by Black men are particularly captivating, and their stories demand attention. My mother frequently reminded me of the value of patience and how essential it is to listen to others for a more rewarding day. While I have my own vision of an ideal day, it's essential to shift our focus to the extraordinary individuals who commit themselves to daily community service. Next, we will hear from Dr. Randall Hall Walker, a man of such dedication.

# Dr. Randall Hall-Walker

Randall Hall-Walker grew up in Detroit, MI, attended MacKenzie High School in 1971, and worked at Chrysler, Pontiac Motors, and Ford Motor Company. In 1982, he turned his life around and began living for the Lord Jesus Christ. He graduated from the Detroit Teen  Challenge in September 1983. Afterward, he left Detroit to attend Trinity Bible College in Ellendale, ND. He married Birdella Wright in 1985, and they toured together, sharing his life story from the streets of Detroit. Today, Randall is Campus President at Freedom Christian University.

Works at FWC Community Development Center as CEO.

Senior Pastor of Freedom Worship Center of Charlotte.

Studied at Trinity Bible College, Cornerstone Christian University-Charlotte. Campus, Saint Thomas Christian University (where he received his honorary doctorate degree), PTP School of Christian Education, and Southeastern University.

Randall lives in Charlotte, North Carolina, with his awesome wife, Dr. Birdella Hall-Walker.

# Pastor Ricou L. Williams

1990 - Times were rough; I was losing another apartment as a result of my drug use. Once again, I didn't know what to do. I felt doomed! After all, I knew I wasn't a bad person, but somehow, I had picked up a habit I could not let go of. My next thought would change my life. I had been raised in the church, and as I began to pray, I asked God to reveal to me why I had been suffering for so many years

under these conditions. I picked up my Bible, "Speak to me," I said. Opening to the first verse I saw; I began to read the words. "All things work together for good; to those that love God and are called according to His purpose!" (Romans 8:28). It all made sense. Everything didn't change at once, but I was on the road to the journey of salvation!

- Under the divine leadership of Pastor Ricou Williams, New Life Purpose Christian Ministries was founded as a vision inspired by God in 1999. Through Jesus, it has been made possible to go into the hedges and highways to preach the word of God, to bring deliverance to the captives, and to open prisons to those who are bound.

Rev. Williams has served the community for years. He has accepted his training under the leadership of several ministries in Charlotte, NC; Burlington, NC; and Tampa, FL. This included Be Encouraged Christian Ministries (in 1995) under the leadership of Pastor Thomas Whitley of Charlotte, NC. There, he served as a pastor assistant/deliverance program. He was later led by God to Deeper Life Christian Ministries (in 1997), where Dr. M.B. Jefferson led him to become a group leader and fundraising pastor for transitional housing programs for recovering alcoholics and addicts. In 1999, Rev. Williams joined Grace Fellowship COGIC, where he preached his trial sermon and became Operations Manager for two transitional housing programs: the Nehemiah House and the House of Ruth. There, he built strong components of ministerial counseling and training as he developed program goals and objectives and planned overall strategies to implement structured operational procedures for the ministry. While at Grace Fellowship COGIC, he was awarded Resident of the Year in 2000. He continued to serve until 2005, when he moved back to Charlotte, NC and began to extend his training and education as a youth counselor at the Timberidge Treatment Facility in Salisbury, NC.

Now that Rev. Williams has developed a greater concept of developmental training and education, he has volunteered his expertise to help other programs in the area, such as The Lighthouse Shelter in Clover, SC, under the leadership of Bishop Samuel Thompson. Rev. Williams is very active in the recovery community, and if you were to discuss his views on his life's journey, you'd often hear him share these words, "...*I grew up in the church; knew of God, but never really knew Him... It only became a time in my life when I had a need for a Savior, that I stretched out my hands, and He met me at the point of my needs!*"

# Lieutenant Commander (Ret) Franklin E. Muhammad

## Medical Service Corps, United States Navy

Born and raised on the West Side of Chicago, Lieutenant Commander Franklin E. Muhammad enlisted in the US Navy in 1991. He completed boot camp and Hospital Corpsman School in San Diego, California. Franklin's first assignment was at the Naval Hospital  Portsmouth, where he served in the Post-Anesthesia Care Unit. In 1993, Franklin reported to the Naval Hospital Yokosuka, Japan, as a general duty corpsman. He worked in five outpatient clinics and the optic fabrication laboratory. Franklin became the first assistant to the ophthalmologist and gynecologist in the operating room. He was one of the founders of the Junior Enlisted Association and served one year as president. Franklin was later transferred to the Branch Health Clinic at Washington Navy Yard in 1998 and began attending the Southern Illinois University Health Care Management degree program. He graduated in 2003 with honors.

Franklin was discharged from the Navy in 2005 and became a Health Services Collegiate Program candidate. He completed his master's in health care management at Marymount University in 2007. He was commissioned as a Lieutenant Junior Grade in the Medical Service Corps, and his first assignment as a Naval Officer was at the Navy Medical Education and Training Command, Bethesda, Maryland.

*Dr. Blanche Penn*

In 2009, Franklin received orders as the Medical Administrative Officer for the USS Enterprise (CVN 65). Their 2011 deployment to the Gulf was during the time of the Osama bin Laden mission in Pakistan. His duties included being Officer of the Deck in Port and Helm Safety Officer during restrictive maneuvering of the ship. Franklin is a qualified Surface Warfare Medical Department Officer.

Following Franklin's tour on the USS Enterprise (CVN 65), he transferred to the U.S. Naval Hospital Yokosuka in 2011 as a Naval Officer. His duties included Department Head, Utilization Management, and Command Fitness Leader. In 2013, Franklin received orders to the NATO Role 3 Multi-National Medical Unit in Kandahar, Afghanistan. His leadership contributed to the team's 98% survival rate of combat casualties. Following his operational assignment, Franklin returned to Yokosuka as Assistant Department Head for Materials Management. His tremendous work ethic led to his promotion to Department Head in 2014 and the Bureau of Medicine's Junior Logistician of the Year.

In 2016, Franklin became the Officer in Charge of the Fourth Medical Logistics Command. Then, in 2018, he graduated with an Executive Master's in Business Administration from the Naval Post Graduate School. His last tour of duty was as Director of Program Operations at TRICARE Area Office Pacific, Okinawa, Japan. He flawlessly executed the TRICARE benefit and host nation's medical care expenses for 190K Active military and family members throughout the Indo-Pacific region.

Personal decorations and military awards include BUMED Junior Logistician of the Year 2014, Surface Warfare Medical Department Officer, Joint Defense Service Commendation Medal,

(3) Navy & Marine Corps Commendation Medals, (3) Navy & Marine Corp Achievement Medals, (4) Navy Good Conduct Medals, National Defense Service Medal, Afghanistan Campaign Ribbon, Global War on Terrorism Expeditionary Medal, Global War on Terrorism Service Medal, Outstanding Volunteer Service Medal, Navy Sea Service Deployment Ribbon, (11) Navy Overseas Service Ribbons, NATO ISAF Medal and Navy Expert Rifle Medal.

# Chris Thompson

Chris Thompson Cultural Ensemble was established in 1991 as a group that focuses on African and African American History. Chris has been dancing, teaching, and producing dance events in Charlotte for over 40 years. He's received numerous awards from CMS, ASEP, NAACP, Mitchell College Inclusion program, Pride Magazine Performance Artist of the Year, Metrolina Theater Award (MTA), Upward Bound Program (JCSU), Creative Loafing Charlotte to name a few.

# Ron Miller

Born in Buffalo New York to the parents of Ronald W Miller and Shirley A miller and have four siblings Michelle, Anthony, Bruce and Cherise. I had a fun and exciting life growing up with a very close knot family. I spent my early summers with my aunt Ruth my dad's sole living sister, her partner Jimmy, and my cousin Ricky who she was raising and was like a big brother to me. I  was always a hard worker at the age of about 6 I would go to the corner supermarket and ask the elderly Ladies if I could carry their groceries to their cars or homes in the neighborhoods it allowed me to have a brown paper bag full of coins which I counted daily. My dad started a new career with law enforcement, and we moved to our first home in an all-white neighborhood we were the only black family within about a 10-block radius. It was the middle of the school year, and I was in the 3rd grade. After school I shoveled neighbors and other small errands. When not working or doing family fun things I spent a lot of time in my room working with my chemistry and biology making formulas and dissecting and breeding various living things as my goal was to become a physician at the time. One of my nicknames in the house was the mad scientist. I initially went to a predominate all-white trade high school which I applied for and was accepted based on scholastic ability and grade point average based on 3 years of junior high school once there I deplored it and found a way to transfer to the cities only all Black high school. I went on to college and changed my major from premed in my sophomore year to Business Management as I was eager to finish school and possibly leave the area.

I moved to Monroe NC and quickly got the first job I could in the mall down the street from where I was residing while working, I met Cassandra a beautiful young Lady very sweet and personable she saw me working in the shoe store through the window and introduced herself to me. Later she introduced me to one of her closest friends, Mae Barrett, who I became close friends with as well. Mae and I started a prayer group and had prayer weekly at her residence in which we feed all those in attendance and feed the less fortunate in the community along with helping with financial needs as much as we were able. I always had vivid dreams but at this point in life I began to write them down when I would wake up from them and thus my first theatrical production HOUSE OF ICHABOD was birthed. None of us had any acting background and several of the cast members were homeless that I used with our first two performance to sold audiences at Blumenthal theater in uptown Charlotte we played there for about two years off and on as the play was in high demand we traveled to other cities and played in major theaters. My next theatrical production was an extension of HOUSE OF ICHANBOD and my third theatrical production THE ONE THAT GOT AWAY was one for the books we had sold out performances for just about every show and was asked on several occasions to hold the show time back due to the extended lines to purchase tickets and for seating as apparently people were sneaking in without purchasing tickets thus creating a seating concern. We traveled to various cities and played in all national theaters as well. Our final performance we played at Booth Playhouse in the Bank of America building in uptown Charlotte to a sold-out audience as

Hamilton was playing at the same time in the adjacent theater. We always gave away free tickets via Radio advertising on the most popular local radio stations in the varies cities we performed. Each show started out with prayer. Covid came and we had to stop performing at which time I started a Youtube Miniseries SACRELIGIOUS DESIRES seasons one and two.

I have always enjoyed helping others and giving back from the successes that I have been blessed to have.

As a thank you R&M Productions to our home base city of Charlotte NC we have an annual Black & White Gala we have catered dinner with a separate salad bar, open bar, door prizes at least 50 percent of attendees win a prize, dancing, fashion show, skit of an upcoming production, and gift card giveaways all for $20 I'm positive that you won't find this anywhere else. I also hit the streets of Atlanta at night to provide blankets, toilet paper, tissue and peanuts to the homeless men and women I see. People ask why not Charlotte I say because Atlanta is where God spoke to my spirit one cold snowy night while visiting to celebrate my God mothers 75th birthday the late DR. Gwendolyn Washington.

Our next theatrical production is Women of God the side Chic which will be hitting stages soon all our performances are made affordable as to be able to share the arts within our community and hopefully inspire, encourage and help others with the content.

Hard work and dedication pay off. God loves a cheerful giver, and I am thankful for the ability to be a cheerful giver even out of my own need at times. On behalf of myself and my company R&M productions I would like to thank my managing partner Mae Barret along with all the cast, musicians, lighting, sound and all our family and supporters. Who would have thought a skinny young man who moved here with $70 and nothing more than a tv and clothes would be able to help so many some may say from rags to suits as God has more than multiplied that $70.

Thank you to Dr. Blanche Penn who has served as our house mother and acted in a few productions please check her out in Sacrilegious Desires as Nurse Beatrice.

To summarize, it is crucial to reassess partnerships and contracts to better support all residents and additional Black male-led organizations. I advocate for increased backing of grassroots groups within the community. Should my understanding be incorrect, I welcome correction. It would be beneficial to acknowledge all grassroots organizations receiving your support, not just the well-known ones but also those burgeoning and in need of assistance. Discussions about potential actions, feasible strategies, necessary measures, and the core objectives are pertinent. The time has come to consolidate our efforts and recognize that these Black men and leaders are actively contributing and making significant strides for the betterment of this community.

# Calvin McCullough

Calvin McCullough was born in Charlotte, North Carolina on October 17, 1951. He was raised in Charlotte and attended West Charlotte High School, graduating in 1969. He attended Business College and received a diploma. He was employed for 36 years with United Parcel Service and 20 years part-time at Merrywood on Park Road. He has been married to  his wife Jacqueline for 49 years and is the father of a daughter Chandra and a son Courtney. He is the grandfather of 4, Jaylah, Ahmir, Camren, and Anniea. He loves his family and the Church. Earlier in life, he was a Sunday School teacher and Junior Trustee at Tabernacle Baptist Church. He is now a member of the Park Church. Calvin has been a mentor to many of his son's friends and always had respect for them and they still love and respect him now as adults. He loves his family, and the grands are the apple of his eye. He loves attending sporting events and family events. He is known for his cooking, especially his fish and buttermilk cornbread. He is active with his alumni class of 1969 of West Charlotte and has served as a volunteer at the school as in previous years when his kids were in elementary, middle, and high school. He served as a volunteer for the first day of school, Father's taking your kids to school on the first day under Dr. Blanche Penn. He is a wonderful husband, father, grandfather, and friend to many. His calm demeanor is a welcoming tool in his quest to serve God.

# Curtis Hayes Jr

Curtis Hayes Jr. is a powerful advocate, mentor, and philanthropist whose life and work embody dedication to the marginalized and the fight for justice. Born in Bluefield, West Virginia, Curtis moved to Charlotte at the age of 12 and graduated from East Mecklenburg High  School. His journey from humble beginnings to becoming a distinguished leader is a testament to his unwavering dedication to the voice of the people.

Curtis's relentless drive and inspirational vision have empowered countless individuals, providing hope and opportunity where it is needed most. As a devoted father to a 9-year-old son and a 14-year-old daughter, he embodies strength, compassion, and leadership, continually paving the way for a more inclusive and equitable future.

Curtis gained global recognition for a powerful, viral message delivered on I-277 during the George Floyd protests. Addressing a young Black man, he urged the creation of a better path forward and highlighted the intergenerational fight for equality spanning three generations. His heartfelt plea resonated worldwide, making the magnitude of the struggle against racial injustice unmistakably clear. Featured on major news outlets like CNN, Good Morning America, BBC, The New York Times, and The Washington Post, Curtis's message became a beacon of hope and a call to action for millions.

A prominent resident of Charlotte and a trailblazing force for change, Curtis is the CEO of Hayes Harmony Innovations, owning The Gook Factory, Rolling Rhythms Ice Cream, and Global Precise Property Services LLC. He is also the founder of EMCB (Excuse Maker or Cycle Breaker) Mentorship, showcasing his deep commitment to nurturing and guiding the next generation. Curtis Hayes Jr. is not just a leader; he is a beacon of empowerment and a catalyst for positive change.

# Gary Mumford

Gary Mumford is a multifaceted individual with a rich background. Here are some key points about him:

## 1. Drummer and Community Advocate:

- Gary Mumford is a talented drummer known for his rhythmic contributions to music and community events.

- He has been involved with the Juneteenth Festival of the Carolinas in Charlotte since its inception in 1997[1].

- Mumford's drumming skills have left a lasting impact, especially during festivals that commemorate Juneteenth[2].

## 2. Shalamar Connection:

- Gary Mumford was the original lead singer of Shalamar, an American R&B and soul music vocal group active since the late 1970s.

- Shalamar's classic lineup included Howard Hewett, Jody Watley, and Jeffrey Daniel, with Mumford as the lead singer initially[3].

- Their hits, including "Take That to the Bank," left a mark on the music scene.

## 3. Body-Popping and Influence:

- Jeffrey Daniel, a member of Shalamar, demonstrated body-popping dance moves on BBC Television's "Top of the Pops," introducing the style to the UK.

- Michael Jackson admired Daniel's dance skills and even co-choreographed Jackson's iconic videos for "Bad" and "Smooth Criminal" from the album Bad[3].

## 4. Community Building and Cultural Awareness:

- Mumford believes that moments like Juneteenth are powerful opportunities for learning, embracing culture, and understanding its significance.

- He hopes that events like Juneteenth will encourage everyone to learn, embrace, and appreciate their cultural heritage[1].

Gary Mumford is a talented drummer known for his contributions to music and community events. Here are some interesting facts about him:

1. **Juneteenth Festival**: Gary Mumford has been involved with the Juneteenth Festival of the Carolinas in Charlotte since its inception in 1997. He's witnessed its growth and evolution over the years, using his drumming skills to celebrate this important holiday[1].

2. **The Djembe**: Gary Mumford is well-versed in playing the Djembe, a West African drum. The Djembe, often called

the "heartbeat," historically served as a messenger, transmitting messages through rhythm. It played a vital role in community events, celebrations, and even daily life, keeping people in tune with nature and each other[1].

3. **Community Building:** Today, Gary Mumford continues to use his drumming to foster community connections. As people reenter society after the pandemic, events like Juneteenth become powerful opportunities for learning, embracing culture, and understanding the significance of traditions like Juneteenth[1].

His passion for music and community engagement shines through, making him an integral part of Charlotte's cultural scene. Gary Mumford's contributions extend beyond music, they touch hearts, build community, and celebrate cultural identity.

# Ronnie Johnson

Ronnie Johnson, a devoted husband, father of three, and grandfather to twins, is a true Charlotte native. He discovered his passion for drawing at the tender age of nine, focusing on sports cars throughout his junior high and high school years.

His artistic journey continued at Winston-Salem State University, where he earned a B.A. in Fine Arts & Studio and developed a deep affection for portrait painting.

"I relish creating portraits that capture people in moments of joy and celebration," he shares.

For the past three decades, Ronnie has been crafting commissioned pieces for family, friends, and colleagues. His preferred medium is oil painting, treasured for its fluid mixing and blending properties. He also works with acrylics, pencils, colored pencils, and pastels. Currently, at 63, Ronnie is gearing up for some of his inaugural exhibitions.

# Darryl L. Johnson Sr.

In Loving Memory
Rest In Peace My Brother
July 19, 1963-July 14, 2024

Darryl grew up in Queen City with his three brothers and four sisters, creating a lively family environment. He attended West Charlotte High School before moving on to UNC Chapel Hill, where he excelled as a football player. Beyond athletics, Darryl possessed a remarkable talent for painting, a skill known to those who knew him well. I proudly display one of his paintings in my home and yearn for the other pieces that capture his essence. Darryl Johnson is a name associated with insurance and community engagement, notably through the Darryl Johnson Agency. Darryl was a devoted member of the Omega Psi Phi Fraternity, Inc., an organization he held dear to his heart. Every time you saw him, he wore something that showcased his pride in his fraternity. A heartfelt thanks to all his fraternity brothers who attended his balloon release and celebration of life. As children grow into adults, we may spread out across the world, sometimes staying in touch, sometimes not knowing everything about our siblings, yet our love for them endures. One truth remains constant: get to know your family, treasure them through the good times and the bad, for they are God's gift to you. With love, here is my poem for you, Darryl. Dr. Blanche Penn

## "Resilience Under the Carolina Sky"

At the core of Charlotte, where towering buildings touch the sky and Southern charm flourishes, Darryl Johnson made his mark. A native son of this vibrant metropolis, he personified its essence: a mix of grit, warmth, and steadfast determination. Darryl's journey commenced on a hot summer's day. The shaded avenues of Charlotte were his childhood arenas, where he pedaled bikes with pals and aspired to reach beyond the urban expanse. His parents, both diligent and gentle, nurtured in him a sense of community and empathy. As he transitioned into adulthood, Darryl's entrepreneurial flame was kindled. He established the Darryl Johnson Agency, tucked away on North Church Street. There, he crafted a haven for families, enterprises, and visionaries. With every client, he instilled a sense of security, tenacity, and optimism. He cherished the freedom of the open road. Life presented its share of challenges, both personal and professional. Darryl weathered adversities involving loss, sorrow, and fortitude. Nonetheless, he remained a steadfast figure against Charlotte's cityscape. Darryl's impact went beyond the confines of his work. It resonated in the joyous laughter at family gatherings, the steady purr of engines on Interstate 77, and the tales exchanged at local cookouts. So, as you relish a glass of iced tea on your porch, think of Darryl Johnson: the protector, the ally, your kin, the steward of aspirations. His narrative, ingrained in the city's heart, gently reminds us: "Through giving, we forge new paths."

# CHAPTER 5

# Pulling It All Together

Uniting all aspects is a vital element of this journey, as these individuals are distinguished members of the community. I take pleasure in informing students, my offspring, adults, and seniors that becoming an inventor is within anyone's reach. This is demonstrated by the many Black male inventors who possess patents and have contributed significantly worldwide. Their inventions profoundly impact our daily lives, both at home and elsewhere. My emphasis lies in engineering, science, and various industries. However, the achievements of these Black Kings have frequently been omitted from historical accounts, inspiring me to author a book that shines a light on more Black Kings of today. It is time we recognize the Black inventors who have shaped history.

**Thomas L. Jennings**: "dry scouring" and the first Black to receive a patent in the United States. If you take the time to read more about what he did with his endeavors, you will develop a deep appreciation for how he chose to utilize his wealth. **Mark E. Dean** was a computer scientist/engineer of hardware that allowed multiple devices like printers, modems, and keyboards to be plugged into a computer. **Garrett Morgan** invented the three-light traffic signal and gas mask. **Lonnie G. Johnson** invented the Super Soaker water gun, which is one of the most popular toys in the United States. Everyone knows **George Washington Carver** has over 100 products made from peanuts. I will name a few of them so you can do a little research on some of the many Black Kings that came before the

Kings today. Percy Lavon Julian, Benjamin Manneker, James Forten, George Peake, Andrew J. Beard, Henry Blair, Hugh M. Browne, Shelby Davidson, Lewis Latimer, Jan Ernst Matzeliger, John Parker, Norbert Rillieux, Samuel Scottron, Lewis Temple, Granville T. Woods, Elijah McCoy, William Harry Barnes, Leonidas Berry, Billy Blanks, Otis Boykin, George Carruthers, Michael Croslin, Meredith Charles Gourdine, Walter Lincoln , Frederick McKinley Jones, Percy Lavon, Julian John King, James Parsons Jr., Edwin Roberts, Alexander Miles, James E. West, Benjamin Boardley, Henry Brown, Alfred L. Cralle, George Franklin Grant, Lloyd Hall, Benjamin Montgomery, Joseph R. Winters, George Crum, George Alcorn, Charles Drew, Leonard C. Bailey, Henry T. Sampson, David N. Crosthwait, Charles Brooks, Jack Johnson Joseph Lee Lloyd Ray, Joseph Dickinson, Matthew Cherry, Richard Bowie Spikes, Robert Pelham, Thomas Mensah, Thomas Stewart, Thomas Elkins, Willis Johnson, John Lee Love, Henry Falkener, Albert C. Richardson, Daniel McCree, Benjamin Thornton, David A. Fisher, Jr. Edward R. Lewis, Joseph Hawkins, Alexander P. Ashbourne, William Binga, James A. Sweeting, Robert R. Reynold, William B. Purvis, Kerrie Holley, John White, **Washington Martin, and Henrietta M. Bradberry.** I was previously unaware of the many Black men who achieved great things before my time, and those who persist in their tireless efforts to uphold the legacy. These leaders have often joined forces to smooth our journey. A salute to all these Kings of the past, present, and future. Peace and blessings to each one.

To summarize, the male participants, referred to as 'destiny males,' would be candid and reliable in sharing their daily contributions to the community. It was crucial for participants to communicate openly and provide unbiased information. The study was delimited to male participation, with the potential limitation being those who were reluctant to disclose their information. Nevertheless, many were forthcoming with their stories. These insights are invaluable for strategic planning aimed at understanding their roles and integration within the community. Evidence and analysis underscore the importance of involvement in any community. Welcome our Kings Forever.

# Appendix A

"Always the Last to know but the First to call when they want something," Dr. Blanche Penn

My sons (Kings Forever)

Felix A. Penn Maldonado

Rafael A. Penn

# Appendix B

Let us take a moment to honor the memory of the great leaders who have departed. Let us dedicate a few minutes to remember our Kings who are no longer among us. May peace and blessings be upon them until we meet again.

# About The Author

**Dr. Blanche Penn**, a dedicated advocate and community leader in Charlotte, North Carolina, has made significant contributions over the years. She is remarkable and has dedicated much of her life to what the late John Lewis aptly termed "good trouble." Her impactful work spans various domains and has left an indelible mark on her community. Here are some notable aspects of her contributions:

## Community Engagement and Advocacy:

Dr. Blanche Penn has been actively participating in local government meetings, advocating for positive change and social justice [23]. She has focused on what the late John Lewis called "good trouble," demonstrating her commitment to social justice and community well-being.

## Community Advocacy:

- She has championed the cause of families affected by unscrupulous landlords, ensuring their rights are protected. (Lake Arbor)

- Her involvement extends beyond policy discussions; she has been a PTA president and even founded a cheerleading squad for seniors. (Silver Fox Cheerleaders)

- She has tirelessly worked to address issues faced by families made homeless due to unscrupulous landlords.

## Authorship:

- Dr. Penn has authored several books, including:

  1. **"Shift Happens"**: A thought-provoking work that delves into personal transformation and resilience [1].

  2. **"The Stay Focused Chronicles"**: An exploration of maintaining focus amidst life's challenges [1].

  3. **"Lake Arbor Home Sweet Home: Charlotte North Carolina Tenant Rights"**: A guide addressing tenant rights in Charlotte, North Carolina [1].

  4. **"Checking Off the Right Box: You Can Always Find Good, but it's a Process"**: A book that encourages finding positivity through life's journey [1].

  5. Greatness Under the Rock – Move that, Rock.

  6. Two new books coming out this fall: "Crown Your King: Make the Best Move" and "The Rock Has Been Removed, and The Queens Have Been Revealed")

## 1. Tenant Rights Advocate:

- Her book titled **"Lake Arbor Home Sweet Home: Charlotte North Carolina Tenant Rights"** suggests her commitment to ensuring fair treatment for tenants in her community[3].

## 2. Passion for Justice:

- Dr. Penn's advocacy work reflects her passion for justice and equity. She actively engages in local government meetings, advocating for the rights of marginalized communities and addressing critical issues[1].

- Her dedication to advocating for families made homeless by unscrupulous landlords demonstrates her deep concern for social justice.

## 3. Community Impact:

- As a member of the **Charlotte Community Think Tank**, Dr. Penn has left a significant impact on her community. Her tireless efforts have made her a respected figure in Charlotte, North Carolina[2].

- Being part of a community-driven organization likely fueled her desire to advocate for positive change.

## 4. Personal Experiences and Empathy:

- Dr. Blanche Penn's books, including **"Shift Happens"** and **"Lake Arbor Home Sweet Home: Charlotte North Carolina Tenant Rights,"** suggest that her personal experiences and empathy play a crucial role in her advocacy[3].

- Perhaps she witnessed injustices firsthand or felt compelled to address issues affecting vulnerable populations.

## 5. Inspiration from John Lewis:

- The late Congressman John Lewis coined the term "good trouble" to describe necessary, nonviolent activism. Dr. Penn's focus on "good trouble" aligns with Lewis's legacy[1].

- Lewis's commitment to civil rights and justice likely inspired Dr. Penn to take action and advocate for positive change.

## 6. Nonprofit Work:

- Blanche Penn is associated with **Winners Plus Inc.**, an organization that focuses on community development and empowerment[2].

- Additionally, she is part of the Mecklenburg Council of Elders, a nonprofit organization that raises awareness of citizens' rights and options, regardless of their past involvement with the law[3].

Dr. Blanche Penn's commitment to community, education, and advocacy continues to positively impact Charlotte, North Carolina. Her commitment to making a difference exemplifies the power of individual action. Let her inspiring journey remind us that even small steps can lead to significant impact. In summary, Dr. Blanche Penn's advocacy journey is fueled by her passion, community impact, personal experiences, and the inspiration she draws from leaders like John Lewis. Her work exemplifies the power of advocacy in creating a better world.

Made in the USA
Middletown, DE
03 September 2024

60280241R00053